Lady Gaga: Imagine Trivia Books
By Lewis King

Question #1

What is the full and original name of lady gaga?

Answer #1

Stefani Joanne Angelina Germanotta.

Question #2

Who is she?

Answer #2

She is an American singer and song writer.

Question #3

When she is born?

Answer #3

She is born on March 28, 1986 and raised in New York City.

Question #4

What is the name of her University where she gets education?

Answer #4

New York University's Tisch School of the Arts.

Question #5

What was her first performance?

Answer #5

She starts performing in the rock music scene of Manhattan's Lower East Side, and was signed with Streamline Records in the end of 2007.

Question #6

What was the first album of Lady Gaga?

Answer #6

The release of her debut album The Fame (2008), make her so famous in the beginning of her career.

Question #7

What was the quality that makes her famous in the world of singing?

Answer #7

The addition of international # 1 singles "Just Dance" and "Poker Face" also make her so attractive singer.

Question #8

Appearance on Billboard magazine?

Answer #8

Lady Gaga has repeatedly appeared on Billboard magazine's Artists of the Year, in the list of 100 Greatest Women in Music.

Question #9

Who signed Lady Gaga in his first album?

Answer #9

Akon find her internal efficiency of vocal abilities in Lady Gaga, on this base Akon signed her to his label Kon Live Distribution.

Question #10

In Which age she start singing in clubs and Bars?

Answer #10

At the age of fourteen Lady Gaga started singing in bars and clubs.

Question #11

Who are Lady Gaga's parents?

Answer #11

Her father's name is Joseph Germanotta he is an internet entrepreneur and her mother's name was Cynthia Germanotta she was working as a telecommunications assistant.

Question #12

In her family which number she have?

Answer #12

In her family Lady Gaga is the elder of two children.

Question #13

What was the background of Lady Gaga's Family?

Answer #13

Lady Gaga stressed that she belongs to a poor family means her family have not a wealthy background.

Question #14

What kind of student?

Answer #14

When she was reading in a high school she was very intelligent, very devoted and much regimented student in her class.

Question #15

Her craze about music was shown in childhood when she was at 4 years?

Answer #15

Lady Gaga initiate playing the piano when she was only 4 years old, she write her first piano ballad at the age of 13 years, and at the age of 14 she also started to perform at open mike nights.

Question #16

What kind of student she was?

Answer #16

Her excitement for musical theatre brought her main roles in high school programs such as Dolls, Philia and Adelaide in Guys in a funny thing happened on the Way to the Forum.

Question #17

Something's about her music career?

Answer #17

After joining CAP 21, they prepared her in music, art, sex and in other related things, they appreciated her songwriting skills. She also wrote many notable thesis on famous pop artists Spencer Tunick and Damien Hirst.

Question #18

What was the most use of Lady Gaga's performance?

Answer #18

The three things which are most used in Lady Gaga's performance are sex, violence, and power.

Question #19

What was her deal with Sony channel?

Answer #19

She signed a deal with Sony/ATV, and starts writing songs for improvement and established acts such as New Kids on the Block, the Pussycat Dolls and Britney Spears.

Question #20

Lady Gaga's musical ideas are valuable?

Answer #20

With deep experiments of her classmates they say's that her musical ideas and images are so admirable, her performance and musical style is the main subject for many and more analysis and scrutiny from critics.

Question #21

What was the message of Perez Hilton about Lady Gaga?

Answer #21

Perez Hilton expressed her message in a clearer way he says that you write really deep intelligent lyrics with superficial concepts.

Question #22

What was her performance in Short Films?

Answer #22

Lady Gaga's music videos are often described as short films. Being challenging is not just about getting people's interest. It's about saying something that truly affects people in a real way, in a positive way.

Question #23

What was Lady Gaga's favorite personalities?

Answer #23

Musically, She greatly influenced By Madonna and Queen, David Bowie, Michael Jackson, she loved and tries to follow these personalities.

Question #24

What was her fastest selling album?

Answer #24

The 1.1 million copies sold in its first week made "Born This Way" the fastest-selling album in 2011.

Question #25

List of popular songs?

Answer #25

- Bad Romance (2009)
- Poker Face (2008)
- Judas (2011)
- Born This Way (2011)
- Telephone (2009)
- Just Dance (1996)
- Alejandro (2005)
- Paparazzi (2008)
- Marry the Night (2011)
- The Edge of Glory (2011)
- Love Game (1996)
- You and I (2011)
- Monster (2009)
- Bloody Mary (2011)
- Hair (2011)

Question #26

What was the Monster Ball Tour?

Answer #26

The success of her album "The Fame Monster (2009)" maker her enable to start the eighteen-month long Monster Ball Tour, later on it becomes the highest-grossing concert tours for her.

Question #27

List of Lady Gaga's Albums?

Answer #27

Unreleased 2012 Lyrics
- A Very Gaga Holiday Lyrics
- Born This Way: The Remix Lyrics
- Born This Way Lyrics
- The Fame Monster Lyrics
- The Fame Lyrics

Made in the USA
Lexington, KY
16 August 2015